D0881001

Death Penalty

Look for these and other books in the Lucent
Overview series:

Death Penalty

by Don Nardo

LUCENT B·O·O·K·S

LUCENT Overview Series

Library of Congress Cataloging-in-Publication Data

Nardo, Don, 1947-
    Death penalty / by Don Nardo.
       p.   cm. — (Lucent overview series)
    Includes bibliographical references and index.
    Summary: Discusses various aspects of the debate over capital
punishment, including its use as a deterrent to crime,
discrimination and the death penalty, juveniles on death row, and
the morality of this sentence.
    ISBN 1-56006-132-4 (alk. paper)
    1. Capital punishment—United States—Juvenile literature.
[1. Capital punishment.]   I. Title.   II. Series.
HV8699.U5N37   1992
364'.66'0973—dc20   92-20366
                                                      CIP
                                                      AC

Contents

INTRODUCTION   7

CHAPTER ONE   11
Past and Present

CHAPTER TWO   25
Does the Death Penalty Deter Crime?

CHAPTER THREE   39
The Risk of Error

CHAPTER FOUR   47
The Death Penalty and Discrimination

CHAPTER FIVE   61
Juveniles on Death Row

CHAPTER SIX   73
Is the Death Penalty Morally Right?

GLOSSARY   84
ORGANIZATIONS TO CONTACT   85
SUGGESTIONS FOR FURTHER READING   89
WORKS CONSULTED   90
INDEX   92
ABOUT THE AUTHOR   96
PICTURE CREDITS   96

Introduction

THROUGHOUT HISTORY, EVERY society has faced the problem of what to do with its worst criminals. Inevitably, societies enacted various laws to deal with this problem. The responsibility for making and enforcing these laws fell on the state, the government ruling over or representing the members of a society. Fines, public humiliation, and imprisonment seemed appropriate punishments for most offenses. However, more serious crimes, such as murder, seemed to warrant more severe punishment. The death penalty, or execution by order of the state, was given to the offenders.

Capital punishment, or the death penalty, has been used since ancient and medieval times. Few people then questioned whether it was justified and necessary. Most societies believed that a criminal should receive punishment proportional to the crime. Ancient writings from around the world express the same sentiment of "an eye for an eye" found in the Bible. People took it for granted that someone who killed should, in turn, be killed. Most societies also believed that such severe punishment was necessary to instill fear in others. Fear of dying would keep someone from committing so serious a crime.

Today, societies still wrestle with the problem

(Opposite page) A British spy is executed during the American Revolution. As did most countries in the eighteenth century, the young United States exacted the death penalty for certain crimes. Although capital punishment still exists in the United States today, many citizens oppose it.

of dealing with their worst criminals. Imprisonment for life remains one standard approach. Most justice systems also try to rehabilitate criminals, that is, restore them to useful, law-abiding lives. Yet despite these approaches, the death penalty continues to be the ultimate form of punishment in most countries.

What differs from earlier ages is that many people no longer accept capital punishment without question. Some people believe that the death penalty is outmoded, a leftover from the uncivilized past. They say that executing criminals is neither justified nor necessary. Execution by the state is just as much murder as one person killing another. Therefore, the death penalty is immoral

A 1928 New York Daily News *headline curtly trumpets the fate of Ruth Brown Snyder and Henry Judd Gray, two convicted murderers executed by the state.*

A work detail leaves a Maryland prison for a work site. Many death penalty opponents believe that executing criminals serves little purpose, while useful employment benefits prisoners and the public.

and should be abolished. At the same time, many other people still support the death penalty. They say that capital punishment is necessary in an imperfect world. The death penalty needs to be retained, they believe, in order to preserve law and order, and therefore society itself.

Thus, many modern societies, including the United States, find themselves in the midst of a moral dilemma. Should the state continue capital punishment when large numbers of people believe it is wrong? And if it does outlaw the death penalty, will serious crimes increase and society be harmed? In an age when people are questioning the wisdom of ancient and time-honored beliefs, many people find these questions unsettling and difficult to answer.

1

Past and Present

THROUGHOUT HISTORY, MANY societies have used capital punishment in one form or another. No one knows exactly which culture first imposed the death penalty. But historians agree that state executions have probably been around for as long as humans have had organized societies. The earliest recorded reference to capital punishment appears in the great law code introduced by King Hammurabi of Babylonia in 2000 B.C. The code ordered the death penalty for a long list of offenses. The list began with the crime of cheating people while selling them beer and continued with more serious crimes, including murder. According to Hammurabi's code, a person could be put to death by burning, drowning, or impalement on sharp stakes.

Punishing crime

The ancient Hebrews were influenced by Babylonian culture, and the Bible has numerous accounts of people being put to death for various crimes or sins. Even in the time of Jesus Christ, death by stoning was the punishment for blasphemy against God or for the sin of adultery.

Other societies also had codes defining capital crimes. However, the presence of a code did not assure that the death penalty would apply equally

(Opposite page) Condemned criminals are pushed off a cliff to be torn apart by a pack of hungry dogs. Many ancient societies used starved lions, dogs, crocodiles, or other beasts as executioners. Such horrific methods were intended to instill fear in the people and thereby deter lawbreaking.

11

to all members of society. In ancient India, the Brahmins were a special group of holy men. They were exempt from execution, even for murder. In the ancient Greek city of Sparta, only slaves received the death penalty. And in colonial America, black slaves sometimes were executed for crimes for which whites were only imprisoned.

The types of crimes punishable by death also varied from group to group. Many societies executed people for murder. But, as in Hammurabi's time, some lesser crimes also resulted in a sentence of death. In ancient Persia, now Iran, a servant who sat on the king's throne while cleaning the throne room was immediately executed. During the 1500s and 1600s, Great Britain often imposed the death penalty. Britain's "Bloody Code," as it was known, listed up to 250 crimes that were punishable by death. These included cutting down a tree, damaging a fish pond, and picking pockets. Because so many crimes in Britain called for the death penalty, there were many executions. Between 1508 and 1547 alone, more than seventy-two thousand people were sentenced to die. After 1837, the British began to limit the

Many societies have punished crimes against religion with death. A medieval woodcut depicts the burning at the stake of John Hus, a Czech religious reformer who was condemned and executed as a heretic in 1415.

In the busy port of Charleston, South Carolina, in 1718, Stede Bonnet was publicly hanged as punishment for piracy on the high seas. His plea for mercy went unheeded. Over the past few centuries, the number of crimes punishable by death in most societies has been sharply reduced.

use of the death penalty and reduced the number of capital crimes to 15.

Throughout history, the death penalty has been carried out in many ways, some of them brutal. Hanging, burning, stoning, and beheading were common in many societies. The Romans executed the condemned by crucifixion, which involved tying or nailing people to crosses. Sometimes the Romans put a person inside a sack with a wild dog or poisonous snake and threw the sack into the river. In ancient Siam, now Thailand,

In a seventeenth-century European town square, a condemned criminal is executed by drawing and quartering. When the horses have stretched his limbs taut, the swordsman hacks them off one by one. Such cruel methods of execution were still in use as recently as the mid-nineteenth century.

capital offenders were thrown into pits filled with starving crocodiles.

The French, Germans, and British of the Middle Ages often boiled people in oil, broke their bones one by one, and flayed them, or stripped their skin, while they were still alive. They also practiced beheading, which became especially popular in France after the guillotine was introduced there in 1792. Another common form of execution in early Europe was "drawing and quartering." In this case, a convicted person's arms and legs were each tied to horses. The horses then ran in opposite directions, tearing the person apart.

Practices such as these were, for the most part, discontinued in Western nations by the mid-nineteenth century. Today, in the United States—one of many nations that still practices capital punishment—the most common methods for executing condemned criminals are electrocution or poisoning with cyanide gas. A few states still use hanging or a firing squad. A new method has recently been adopted by some states: lethal injection. In this method, a deadly drug is introduced intravenously into the condemned person's bloodstream. Death is quick, peaceful, and painless. This method is seen to be more humane than electrocution, gassing, or hanging.

Federal cases

Death sentences in the United States can be imposed by either the federal government or the states. Under federal law, several crimes are punishable by death. One is treason, or betraying the country. Other federal capital offenses include deserting the armed forces during wartime, murder committed by a soldier, kidnapping and murder

A photograph of the 1865 hanging of those found guilty of conspiring to assassinate Abraham Lincoln. Today, the death sentence is rarely imposed for federal crimes.

President George Bush supports increasing the number of federal crimes for which the death penalty can be imposed. Many politicians today believe the death penalty is an effective deterrent to serious crime.

that involves crossing state lines, and murder committed during an airplane hijacking.

Federal death penalty cases are rare, in large part because the crimes considered capital offenses under federal law are not very common. By the middle of 1992, for example, only six inmates were awaiting execution for federal crimes.

Some U.S. lawmakers believe that federal death penalty laws are too lenient. In 1991, two legislators introduced bills in Congress to increase the number of federal crimes punishable by death to more than fifty. These included attempted murder, attempted assassination of the president, and dealing in illegal drugs. Backed by President George Bush, those in favor of the bills argued that the American public is concerned about the country's increasing crime rate. They claimed that an expanded list of capital offenses would deter, or discourage, crime. The fear of eventual execution, the bills' backers said, would stop many would-be criminals from committing crimes. After much discussion, the proposed laws did not pass, mainly because legislators from several states could not agree on certain technical provisions in the laws. But the backers of these laws hope to reintroduce them at a later date.

The states

While federal cases involving the death penalty are rare, death sentences on the state level are more common. Thirty-six states have laws allowing the death penalty. State laws at the present time consider only one crime, murder, to be a capital offense. Not all murder cases, however, end in capital punishment. States usually impose death sentences for murders committed during the course of other serious crimes, such as rape.

During the 1980s, the states sentenced about 300 people to death each year. Most of these people are still awaiting execution. From 1988 to 1991, for example, more than 2,000 inmates were housed each year on death row. In 1991, the highest number of death row occupants on record—2,547—awaited execution in state prisons.

This number is so high because it often takes many years to exhaust all the appeals each convict has the right to make. The appeals process is very complex and time-consuming. But to protect the constitutional rights of each inmate, every appeal possible is made to the courts to ascertain whether the death sentence is indeed warranted.

Inmates who can show that they were wrongly convicted of a crime or improperly sentenced to die are released from prison or given a lesser sentence. Depending on the circumstances, a lesser sentence may mean brief imprisonment or impris-

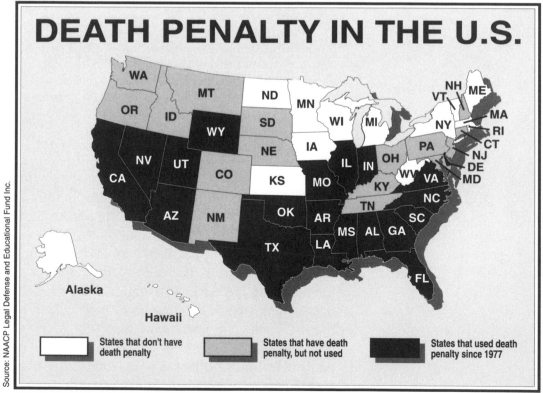

Source: NAACP Legal Defense and Educational Fund Inc.

onment for a lifetime. When all appeals fail, however, inmates sentenced to die eventually face execution. Between 1976 and the middle of 1992, 161 executions took place in states with death penalty laws.

Making a strong statement

States that continue to use the death penalty believe that it is moral, constitutional, and an effective punishment and deterrent to murder. They want to make a strong statement to would-be murderers that the consequences of taking human life are serious. Those who violate the rights of others should expect to lose their own rights—even to live. Such a position has often been taken by those whose philosophy shaped free societies like the United States. Nineteenth-century English philosopher and reformer John Stuart Mill, for instance, stated:

> Does fining a criminal show want of respect for property, or imprisoning him, for personal freedom? Just as unreasonable is it to think that to take the life of a man who has taken that of another is to show want of regard for human life. We show, on the contrary, most emphatically our regard for it, by the adoption of a rule that he who violates that right in another forfeits it for himself, and that while no other crime that he can commit deprives him of his right to live, this shall.

For many states it is an economic matter as well. They believe it unjust to spend the hundreds of thousands of dollars a year it takes to keep a convict in prison for life. That money could be better used, they argue, for programs to help law-abiding citizens. There is disagreement, however, over which costs more: execution or life imprisonment. Some studies indicate that execution actually costs more when all legal appeals are figured into the equation. Costs may also differ from state to state.

STATES WITH MOST EXECUTIONS SINCE 1965

Texas 43
Florida 27
Louisiana 20
Georgia 15
Virginia 13

Source: National Coalition to Abolish the Death Penalty.

Not all states have death penalty laws. Since the mid-1800s, fourteen states have abolished capital punishment. Among these are Wisconsin, Iowa, Massachusetts, Rhode Island, Alaska, New York, and West Virginia. These states did away with the death penalty because they believed it to be an overly cruel form of punishment. When Rhode Island abolished capital punishment in 1852, Governor Dennis J. Roberts expressed the view that the death penalty was a leftover from an earlier, more brutal, and less-civilized justice system. He said:

> The death penalty . . . was most readily invoked [imposed] in that by-gone era when prisons were places of hopeless confinement and when torture and abuse of those convicted of even petty crimes were an accepted norm.

Besides the United States, 143 other countries presently have the death penalty. Of these, at least 18 use the penalty strictly for special offenses against the state, most often treason, or the be-

The rogues' gallery. These teenagers were executed in nineteenth-century New York for petty crimes like pickpocketing and burglary. Modern-day New York, judging the death penalty too cruel for any crime, has abolished capital punishment.

HIGHWAYMAN AT 17

BURGLAR AT 17

MURDERER AT 19
HANGED AT THE TOMBS

PICKPOCKET AT 15

BURGLAR AT 18

HIGHWAYMAN AT 15

PICKPOCKET AT 13

HIGHWAYMAN AT 15

trayal of one's country. These countries include England, Argentina, Canada, Israel, Mexico, Italy, Spain, New Zealand, and Switzerland.

Some 126 other countries impose the death penalty for treason and murder. Among these are Chile, China, Cuba, Egypt, India, Japan, Kuwait, Libya, Poland, Turkey, and Vietnam.

The death penalty is also used in some countries for crimes other than treason and murder. In Kenya, located in western Africa, execution is mandatory for anyone who commits robbery while carrying a dangerous weapon, even if that weapon is not used. In Jordan, in the Middle East, a death sentence is mandatory for someone who rapes a girl under the age of fifteen.

A few countries, such as Iraq and China, impose the death penalty for political crimes. These

often include belonging to organizations condemned by the government, printing antigovern-
ment opinions, and publicly insulting the nation's
leader. By imposing capital punishment for such
political crimes, the leaders of these countries
hope to exert strong control over the way people
act and express themselves. These countries also
impose the death penalty for many other crimes.
For example, Iraq imposes the death penalty for
attempted murder, theft, bribery, and forgery, or
making false documents, in addition to treason,
murder, and political crimes. China imposes the
death penalty for robbery, stealing from one's
employer, government corruption, bribery, smug-
gling, drug-trafficking, assault and battery, leading a criminal gang, forcing a woman into prosti-
tution, and many other crimes.

Because information about executions is not
freely available from countries like Iraq and
China, it is difficult to confirm the exact number
of executions each year. But according to
Amnesty International, a human rights organization that opposes capital punishment, at least five
hundred Chinese were executed between 1985
and 1988. Amnesty and other groups estimate
that more than six hundred executions occurred
in Iraq each year during the 1980s. These execution totals were unusually high when compared
with the figures from most other countries. More
typical were Poland, which executed only eleven
people between 1985 and 1988, Japan with nine
executions, Kuwait with six, and Romania with
two.

Abolishing executions

Although many executions do occur around the
world each year, the use of the death penalty is by
no means universal. At least thirty-five countries
have abolished capital punishment for all crimes.

Death Penalty Around the World

(Figures represent number of countries)

44

16

106

21

■ Executions carried out within past 10 years

■ Abolished

■ Abolished for all but exceptional crimes, such as war crimes

□ No executions in 10 years or more

Source: *Los Angeles Times.*

Among these are Australia, Costa Rica, Finland, France, Germany, Haiti, Iceland, Norway, Panama, Sweden, and Venezuela. The last executions in Finland took place in 1942, in Australia in 1967, and in France in 1977.

The reasons given by these nations for not using the death penalty are generally the same. First, they express the belief that the death penalty does not deter someone from committing a crime. They say that while in the act of committing crimes, few criminals seriously consider the possibility of eventual execution. Therefore, it makes no sense to argue that fear of execution keeps the crime rate down.

The second reason cited by these nations for abolishing the death penalty is the belief that execution is morally wrong. No one, they say, including the state, has the right to take a human life. This point of view was summed up by the noted French writer and Nobel prize winner Albert Camus in the 1940s and 1950s. Camus spoke forcefully against the death penalty, calling it nothing more than society's expression of primitive revenge. Camus and other leading French writers helped sway public opinion against capital punishment in France. French legislators abolished executions of all kinds in 1981. Norway took a similar stand when it abolished the death penalty for all offenses in 1979. The Norwegian government called capital punishment "inhumane" and stated its hope that its stand against executions would create an example for other countries.

A major difference exists between the positions of the countries that have abolished the death penalty and those that still practice it. Yet in nearly all countries, whether or not executions are allowed, the issue of capital punishment remains controversial and emotional. Around the world, the use of the death penalty inspires strong personal opinions and provokes heated arguments. And the controversy over whether the state should kill is likely to continue well into the twenty-first century.

The writings of famed author Albert Camus and others turned French public opinion against capital punishment. France abolished the death penalty in 1981.

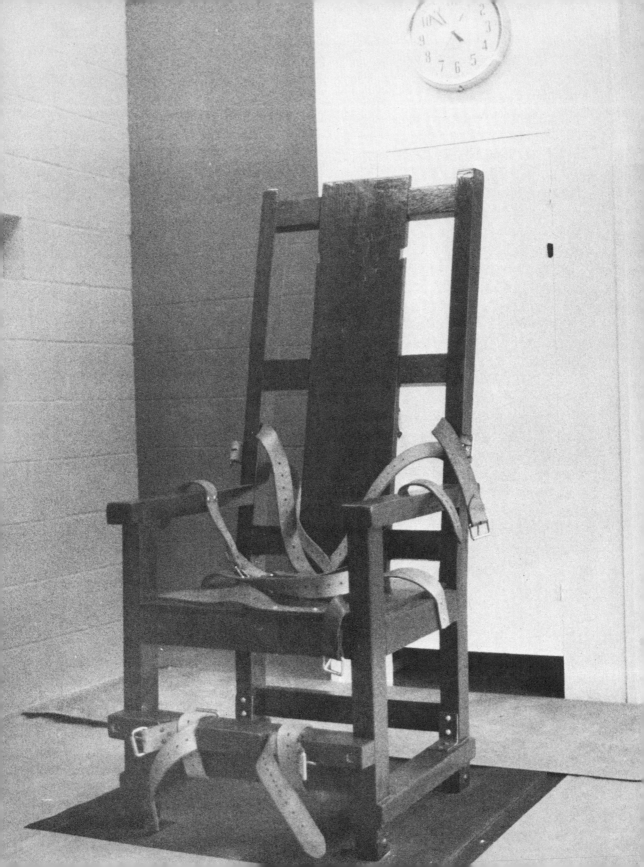

2

Does the Death Penalty Deter Crime?

ONE OF THE most important and hotly debated issues surrounding the death penalty is the idea of deterrence. For centuries, supporters of capital punishment have said that fear of receiving the death penalty keeps many people from committing murder and other serious crimes. In this way, the death penalty helps safeguard society. As far back as 1701, some British lawmakers argued before Parliament, "Those [criminals] who shew [show] no mercy should find none; and if Hanging will not restrain them, Hanging them in chains, and starving them, or . . . breaking them on the Wheel, or Whipping them to Death . . . should."

Today, death penalty advocates believe that the threat of execution is still a powerful deterrent. Norman Darwick, of the International Association of Chiefs of Police, summed up this point of view in a speech to the U.S. Senate in 1981. "The more systematically we eliminate murderers by executions," said Darwick, "the greater will be the reinforcement against killing and the greater the number of innocent lives saved."

(Opposite page) The electric chair was introduced in the early twentieth century as a more humane form of execution. Today, however, it is considered by many to be cruel. Some proponents believe that the prospect of "getting the chair" deters would-be criminals.

25

Opponents of capital punishment have argued just as strongly that the death penalty in no way stops people from committing crimes. "The punishment of death has never prevented determined men from injuring society," said Italian criminologist Cesare Beccaria in 1764. Still inspired by Beccaria's arguments, today's death penalty opponents say there is no conclusive evidence that the death penalty deters crime. Howard Zehr, a leader of the U.S. Mennonite Church, has said, "If the death penalty deters, the deterrent effect is so small that even the most sophisticated attempts have been unable to measure it."

Measuring deterrence

Measuring the death penalty's effect on crime is no easy task. Many factors besides the threat of execution can influence crime rates. For example, the easy availability of handguns or increased violence among street gangs might lead to a higher number of murders. Strict gun controls or the absence of street gangs might lead to fewer murders. For this reason, it is difficult to show a direct link between the death penalty and crime. Even if all other factors could be eliminated, measuring deterrence would still be difficult. There is no way to know how many people did not commit a murder because they feared eventual execution.

Nevertheless, if the death penalty does deter murder, its effect on murder rates should be measurable in some way. Some opportunities to test the deterrence theory have arisen in the United States in recent years. For nearly two centuries, people had measured crime rates when the death penalty was routinely carried out. Then from 1968 to 1976, states across the country halted executions while the U.S. Supreme Court heard a case that challenged the constitutionality of the

death penalty. While the executions were stopped, researchers could see if crime rates changed.

During the moratorium, or temporary suspension, on capital punishment, researchers gathered murder statistics across the country. Believers in deterrence felt that the statistics proved their theory. As researcher Karl Spence of Texas A&M University points out, in 1960 there were 56 executions in the United States and 9,140 murders. By 1964, when there were only 15 executions, the number of murders had risen to 9,250. In 1969, there were no executions and 14,590 murders, and in 1975, after six more years without executions, 20,510 murders occurred. According to Spence, this shows that the number of murders grew as the number of executions shrank. Thus, he claims, the deterrent effect of capital punish-

Gun control advocates publicly demonstrate their belief that gun ownership causes violent crime. Like gun control, the death penalty may affect the rate of murder and other violent crime, but just how much is hard to measure.

ment was lost during the years when no one was executed. Spence says:

> While some [death penalty] abolitionists try to face down the results of their disastrous experiment and still argue to the contrary, the . . . [data] concludes that a substantial deterrent effect has been observed . . . In [any given] six months, more Americans are murdered than have died by execution in this entire century. . . . Until we begin to fight crime in earnest [by using the death penalty], every person who dies at a criminal's hands is a victim of our inaction.

The Utah statistics

Another opportunity to test the deterrent effect of capital punishment arose in Utah during the 1970s and 1980s. Researchers gathered murder statistics around the time of three well-publicized executions. They wanted to see if murder rates rose or dropped after the executions. On January 17, 1977, Gary Gilmore was executed by a firing squad at the Utah State Prison. During the year before Gilmore died, 55 murders occurred in Utah, a rate of 4.5 per 100,000 people. In 1977, after the execution, 44 murders occurred, a rate of 3.5 per 100,000. That was a 20 percent decrease in the murder rate. A similar situation occurred in 1987 when Utah executed Pierre Dale Selby for murder. Between January and August of that year, Utah experienced 38 murders, a monthly average of 4.75. Between September and December, the months following Selby's death, there were 16 murders, a monthly average of 4.0 and a 16 percent decrease. During the six-month period following the execution of Arthur Gary Bishop on June 10, 1988, Utah showed a 19 percent drop in the murder rate.

In each of these cases, the murder rate in Utah temporarily decreased as the execution neared and then took place. According to Robert W. Lee,

An anti-death penalty demonstrator expresses his views with a large sign in front of the U.S. Supreme Court after justices rejected last minute requests to block the execution of Gary Gilmore.

a contributing editor to the conservative magazine *The New American*, these decreases are evidence of deterrence. As death became more of a reality as a punishment for murder, Lee believes, people in Utah were deterred from committing murder. "To be sure," says Lee, "there are other variables that could have influenced the results, but the figures are there and [death penalty] abolitionists to date have tended simply to ignore them."

Other variables

The existence of other variables, however, is precisely what causes some researchers to question whether there is a direct link between the death penalty and crime rates. They believe it is nearly impossible to measure which factors affect people's behavior and by how much. Therefore, hard evidence linking capital punishment to murder rates is lacking. Some researchers claim there is no direct evidence that people who committed murders during the execution moratorium did so because there was temporarily no death penalty. And likewise, no direct evidence exists that people refrained from killing in Utah because executions were taking place. In other words, perhaps some other factors, and not these three executions, caused the decreases in Utah's murder rates.

What are some of the factors that might lead to decreases or increases in murder rates? Some researchers, like American criminologist John P. Conrad, point out that social and economic fac-

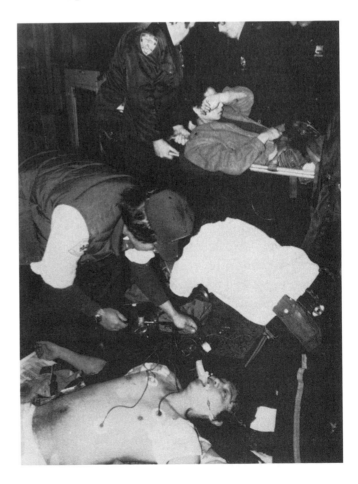

Gang violence is one of the many factors that affect murder rates.

tors play a part. During periods of social turmoil and economic instability, says Conrad, violent crimes like assault and murder tend to increase. This is because desperate, angry, unhappy people are more likely to take out their frustrations on others. Explains Conrad, "The race riots of the 1960s, the Vietnam War, the growing instability of the economy must have had their effect on the crime rates—effects to which numbers cannot be assigned." Similarly, poverty and lack of jobs in the nation's inner cities lead many young people to join street gangs. Murders committed by gang members add significantly to local and national murder rates. Other factors, such as drug-related violence and the growing availability of firearms also may contribute. Regarding murder rates in general, says Conrad, "it is impossible to conclude that capital punishment . . . [has] anything to do with it."

The Canadian and Swiss experiences

As cited by Karl Spence and Robert Lee, murder rates increased during the execution moratorium and decreased directly after the Utah executions. The figures, argue these researchers, show that a link exists between the death penalty and murder rates. But murder statistics do not always suggest such a link. In fact, statistics gathered from several foreign countries that have abolished the death penalty for most or all crimes seem to show just the opposite. These countries report no increases in murders following a ban on capital punishment. Some even show fewer murders committed after abolishing executions.

Canada, for example, abolished the death penalty for murder in 1976, keeping it only for such crimes as treason and mutiny during times of war. The murder rate in Canada decreased after the death penalty for murder was eliminated.

In 1976, there were 561 murders in Canada, a rate of 2.43 per 100,000 people. By 1980, the number of murders had declined to 459, a rate of 1.92. John Conrad says:

> Note that . . . there has been a decline in the incidence of murder and in the rate per 100,0000 [people]. I am not so simple as to suppose that the abolition of capital punishment was responsible for the decline. . . . It is at least possible that increasingly strict control of firearms is partly responsible for the decline in the number of murders. . . . But however we account for the course of the homicide [murder] rates, it is unarguable that they have not been increased by the 1976 legislation. If there were anything of substance to the . . . [deterrence argument], we would expect a sharp increase in the number of murders and the rates of their commission.

The situation in Switzerland, which ended capital punishment for murder in 1942, was similar. Although the Swiss did not see a decrease in murder or other crime rates, they also did not see an increase. A later report by the Swiss government stated that "the complete abolition of the death penalty in Switzerland . . . [has] not resulted in an increase in the number of homicides or the volume of crimes in general."

Crimes of passion

Some people maintain that a better way of determining the deterrent effect of executions is to examine the state of mind of murderers. Do people, when thinking about or committing murder, actually consider that they might later be executed for the act? Statistics show that most murders in the United States are crimes of passion. These are crimes committed by a person who is emotionally upset, enraged, or temporarily out of control. Says Howard Zehr, most murders are not planned in advance and, while committing them, people are too emotionally carried away to think

about the consequences. Zehr explains:

> Some crimes, such as tax evasion, involve consid-
> erable rational planning, and deterrence may have
> relevance to them. What we know about murder,
> however, indicates that most homicides are acts of
> passion, impulsive acts committed under tremen-
> dous stress and/or the influence of alcohol or
> drugs by individuals prone to aggressive, impul-
> sive behavior. . . . These people do not make ratio-
> nal calculations of pain and gain at the time of
> their acts.

Thus, Zehr says the threat of capital punishment has no deterrent effect in most murders.

Planned crimes

Unfortunately, psychiatrists and other authorities know very little about how much the threat of
punishment deters rationally committed crimes.

Some studies show that capital punishment deters crime. Other studies indicate this is not the case. These conflicting results fuel continued debate between death penalty supporters and opponents, two of whom discuss the issue outside of California's San Quentin State Prison.

Only a few studies have tried to measure the direct influence of the death penalty on violent offenders who did consider the death penalty before committing their crimes. These studies have yielded conflicting results. For example, the Los Angeles Police Department conducted a study in 1970 and 1971 in which statements of violent criminals were gathered. About 50 percent of the criminals reported that fear of the death penalty deterred them from carrying weapons or loaded guns while committing their crimes. Just 10 percent of those interviewed said that they would kill whether or not capital punishment existed. This seems to show that the death penalty acted as a deterrent in a majority of these cases.

In contrast, other interviews with convicted murderers have suggested that many who planned their murders in advance did not worry about later suffering the death penalty. For example, writer and influential death penalty opponent Eugene B. Block reports the case of a prison chaplain who talked to many convicted murderers when Britain still performed executions. Of 167 murderers on Britain's death row, 164 said that they had witnessed at least one execution before they committed their crimes. Yet, they acted anyway. This seems to show that the offenders did not fear execution enough for it to deter them.

In fact, says Block, many criminals believe that they are too clever even to get caught, much less be executed. "Experienced criminals consider themselves safe from capture," Block claims, "and therefore from punishment. There is no fear of punishment in their minds." There is some circumstantial evidence supporting this view, as reported by writer Elinor Horwitz in her book *Capital Punishment, U.S.A.*:

> During the almost three hundred years when pickpocketing was a capital offense in England, pickpockets were invariably found among the crowds at the gallows. As soon as preparations for the hanging became exciting and the audience became absorbed in the show, they went into action. The scene in no way deterred them from committing a capital offense.

A brutalizing effect?

While the arguments about deterrence continue, it is important to note that some evidence suggests that the death penalty actually increases violent crime. "Rather than preventing violence," Howard Zehr says, "capital punishment may have a 'brutalizing effect' that increases the level of violence in our society. It may raise, not lower, murder rates." According to Zehr:

Some potential killers see executions as evidence that lethal vengeance is justified. . . . They learn from these executions that it is acceptable to eliminate someone who wrongs them. . . . The example of a life for a life may actually cheapen life, not increase its value.

Dr. Louis West of the Department of Psychiatry at the University of California, Los Angeles Medical Center agrees. Says West, "Legal extermination of human beings in any society generates a profound tendency among the citizens to accept killing as a solution to human problems." For example, West believes that some troubled people feel their own death will end their problems. They cannot face suicide, so they purposely kill in order to get the state to execute them. "These murders are . . . perpetrated in an attempt to commit *suicide* by committing *homicide*," West explains. He lists many examples of murderers requesting or insisting upon the death

Anti-death penalty protestors hold a vigil outside of San Quentin in April 1992. They were expressing their opposition to the execution of Robert Alton Harris, a convicted murderer.

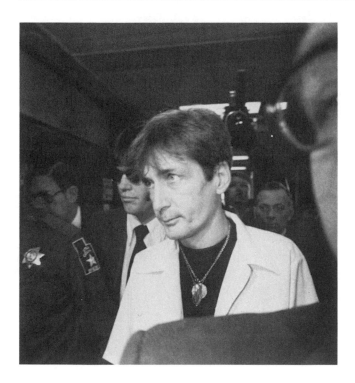

Gary Gilmore, convicted in Utah of murder, attracted national attention in 1977. Gilmore insisted that he be executed for his crime. Death penalty opponents claim that, rather than deterring Gilmore, Utah's death penalty law may have played a part in Gilmore's decision to kill.

penalty. One of the most well known of these cases was that of Utah murderer Gary Gilmore. All through his trial, Gilmore stated that he wanted to be executed. Says West:

> I believe this to be a significant reason for the tendency to find proportionally more homicides in death penalty states than in those without it. I even know of cases where the murderer left an abolitionist state deliberately to commit a meaningless murder in an executionist state.

Whether or not the death penalty actually deters crime remains unclear. Opponents of executions feel their view has been proven by the available evidence. Advocates of capital punishment disagree. They contend that the same evidence and statistics show the opposite. As this heated debate rages, each side continues to present its case and challenge the other side to disprove it.

3

The Risk of Error

(Opposite page) James Richardson is overcome with grief at the funeral services for his seven murdered children. Richardson's world fell apart when he lost his children, but that was only the beginning of his nightmare: He was later convicted of their murders and sentenced to die. His innocence was finally proved after he endured twenty-one years on death row.

FEW DEATH PENALTY issues are as emotionally charged as the possible execution of an innocent person. The U.S justice system is not perfect, nor are the people who work in it. Like anyone else, police, prosecutors, defense lawyers, and judges make mistakes. Some mistakes are unintentional, and some come from carelessness or dishonesty. Whatever the cause, people are sometimes accused, tried, and sentenced for crimes they did not commit.

This is a primary concern of those who oppose the death penalty. Death penalty opponents believe that the possibility of killing an innocent person is reason enough to end all capital punishment. They recall the words of eighteenth-century British lawmaker William Blackstone: "It is better that ten guilty persons escape than one innocent suffer."

Those who support the death penalty do not wish to see an innocent person die either. They point out that the execution of an innocent person rarely happens in the United States, especially in recent history. The legal system has a number of safeguards to ensure that only the guilty are punished.

One of these safeguards is the right to an

Eighteenth-century British statesman William Blackstone opposed the death penalty and his comments are often quoted by death penalty opponents.

attorney. The state cannot prosecute and condemn a person unless that person is represented by a certified lawyer. Another safeguard is the requirement that all the members of a jury vote for the death penalty. This ensures that the jurors are absolutely convinced that the defendant deserves the death penalty. If just one juror remains doubtful, a death sentence cannot be imposed. Also, in death penalty cases the right of appeal to a higher court is automatic. That means that every condemned criminal's case will be reviewed by another judge. During the appeals process, which is usually lengthy, the convicted person has the opportunity to gather additional evidence to help overturn the conviction or at least reduce the sentence.

As long as safeguards such as these are in place, minimizing the risk of error, capital punishment is a fitting penalty for so grievous a crime as murder, death penalty advocates believe. They cite the comments of nineteenth-century

British political philosopher John Stuart Mill, who said:

> This would be indeed a serious objection if these miserable mistakes [executions of the innocent] . . . could not be made extremely rare. . . . But in so grave a case as that of murder, the accused, in our system, has always the benefit of the merest shadow of a doubt.

No one knows for certain how many innocent people have been executed. Amnesty International has reported the results of one survey, which studied capital murder cases in the United States between 1900 and 1985. The survey found that 23 innocent people were executed during that time. The same survey revealed that "the discovery of new evidence resulted in acquittal, pardon, commutation [reduction] of sentence or dismissal of the charges . . ." for 327 others.

These numbers are powerful testimony to two sides of the U.S. justice system: its effectiveness

Gladys Owens wipes a tear from her eye during a news conference held upon the release from prison of her son Aaron. Aaron Owens spent eight years on death row for a murder he did not commit. Because of the appeals process built into the U.S. justice system, Aaron's innocence was finally proved and his life spared.

and its flaws. The complex and often agonizingly slow workings of the justice system usually succeed but sometimes fail.

Cases in which an innocent person was sentenced to die are few, but those that are known illustrate how this situation can occur. Most of the time the cause is human error or lack of skill in pleading or judging a case. In some cases, however, the innocent person's conviction and sentence result from willful wrongdoing by law enforcement officers or other authorities. This is what happened in the case of James Richardson.

Justice gone wrong

James Richardson was convicted of murder in 1968 and sentenced to die in Florida's electric chair. His innocence was later proved, and he was released—but not before he had spent twenty-one years on death row awaiting execution for a crime

James Richardson and his wife, Annie Mae, arrive at the Florida courthouse where he would begin the legal process that would go astray, resulting in a wrongful conviction and his near-execution. A concerned attorney and the court appeals process saved Richardson's life.

he did not commit. His conviction and sentence are an unfortunate example of justice gone wrong. Richardson, it was later revealed, had been the victim of lies, deceit, and poor legal representation.

Richardson, a poor, black farm worker, had been convicted of killing his seven children. The children had been poisoned while their parents worked in the fields. Richardson was arrested and charged with their murders.

Authorities said Richardson's motive was to collect the money from his children's life insurance policies. At the trial, three jail inmates testified that Richardson had confessed his guilt to them. But no one, including Richardson's court-appointed lawyer, stated during the trial that Richardson could not have collected the insurance money. The insurance policies had lapsed. Neither did anyone mention at the trial that the sheriff had promised the three inmates reduced jail time in exchange for their testimony.

In addition, a prosecutor withheld more than nine hundred pages of evidence that could have brought out important information. This information included unusual details about one of Richardson's neighbors. The neighbor had served four years in prison for killing her second husband, and her first husband had died mysteriously after eating a meal she had prepared for him. She had been admitted to a nursing home after the murders at the Richardson's. She confessed to staff members there that she had killed the children. But the staff said nothing about her comments.

An innocent man spared

After these and other details appeared in newspapers, the authorities reopened the case. They concluded that the neighbor, not Richardson, had poisoned the children. Richardson was released.

An innocent man had been spared execution.

Philosophy professor Lloyd Steffen of Northland College in Ashland, Wisconsin, says:

> What the Richardson case points out is that the death penalty always holds the potential for interfering mightily with justice. In the Richardson case, guilt lies with the accusers, and the irrevocable [final] nature of the death penalty would have prevented Richardson from receiving . . . [the] justice he finally did receive. Despite being the result of a legal process, his death would have constituted an unjustified killing—an actual murder.

But many who support the death penalty would argue that society must risk an occasional mistake in order to see that justice is done. Such was the opinion of a U.S. Senate committee that was reviewing the death penalty laws in 1981. The committee's chairman, South Carolina senator Strom Thurmond, stated "that this minimal risk [of executing innocents] is justified by the protection afforded to society by the death penalty."

Death penalty supporters also contend that the realty of human limitations and malice is unfortunate, but it does not negate the value and effectiveness of a system with such a high success rate. After all, because of the legal system, James Richardson's case was reopened, and he was proved innocent. The system condemned him and the system later acquitted him.

An imperfect world

The fallibility of the justice system, and the irreversibility of the death penalty, together fuel continued concern among those who oppose capital punishment. The American Civil Liberties Union (ACLU), a nonprofit political organization, summed up this viewpoint in 1981. Stated the ACLU:

> Death is a punishment absolute. Final. There are no more appeals. No reversals. It is an irrevocable [permanent] punishment carried out by a criminal justice system that is far from perfect. And can never be perfect, as long as it is run by human beings.

Those who support the death penalty, for the most part, view it as a necessary tool in an imperfect world even if the process does not always work as it should. One U.S. Senate report stated this position this way:

> All that can be expected of . . . [human authorities] is that they take every reasonable precaution against the danger of error. . . . If errors are then made, this is the necessary price that must be paid within a society which is made up of human beings.

Society, then, must ultimately decide whether it prefers to take a risk and keep the death penalty or avoid it and abolish the death penalty. It is a difficult decision to make.

Senator Strom Thurmond chaired the Senate committee that stated that the possibility of mistakenly executing an innocent person is a necessary price to pay for protection from crime.

4

The Death Penalty and Discrimination

AMERICA'S DEATH ROWS are filled with people who have lived much of their lives in poverty. Nearly half of these inmates are black or Latino. Michael Endres, a criminal justice professor at Xavier University in Cincinnati, Ohio, testifies to this. He states:

> What is particularly disquieting . . . is that a disproportionately large number of [death penalty] cases involve blacks and almost all of them involve the poor. . . . Case studies on death row inmates indicate that whatever their racial origins, the condemned are invariably society's losers. They are poorer, less educated, if not less intelligent, less employable.

In 1973, the U.S. Supreme Court ruled that courts were discriminating against certain classes and races of people when applying the death penalty. Justice William O. Douglas wrote:

> The discretion [judgement] of judges and juries in imposing the death penalty enables the penalty to be selectively applied, feeding prejudices against the accused if he is poor and despised and lacks political clout, or if he is a member of a suspect or unpopular minority.

(Opposite page) Nearly half of the inmates who fill death row are black or Latino, raising questions about the death penalty and discrimination.

47

Children play amidst the garbage in a New York City slum. Death penalty opponents believe that the death penalty is unjust because it discriminates against the poor.

A life in poverty may contribute to the disproportionate number of poor people on death row. However, many researchers believe this high number is not the result of poverty alone. In various ways, they say, the justice system itself discriminates against those without money. A person with money can hire the best lawyers. Those without money often are represented by young, less-experienced lawyers, overloaded public defenders, or court-appointed lawyers who have little interest in the case.

They are divided, however, about whether these inequalities are the result of discrimination. Some death penalty advocates, for example, point out that the high number of poor people on death rows is better explained by examining who commits the crimes. States Ernest van den Haag,

"Most murders are committed by poor persons, often during robberies. The wealthy rarely murder, just as they rarely commit burglaries, for obvious reasons."

Racial bias

Just as the number of poor people on death row has raised questions about discrimination, so has the number of ethnic minorities there. In 1992, just over 1,300, or about 51 percent, of death row inmates in the United States were white. About 1,170, or 46 percent, were black or Latino. These numbers show that there are fewer minorities than whites on death row. However, researchers then compared these figures with the number of whites, blacks, and Latinos in the general population. The comparison showed that blacks and Latinos are found on death row and are executed in greater proportions than they appear in the general population. For instance, of the 161 inmates executed between 1976 and 1992, about 44 percent were black or Latino. Yet blacks and Latinos make up only about 16 percent of the general population.

L. J. Kern by permission of *The Guardian*.

These numbers can be interpreted several ways. Advocates of capital punishment suggest that the disproportionate numbers may have more to do with who commits capital crimes than with racial bias in sentencing. For example, Frank Carrington, author of *Neither Cruel nor Unusual*, says that "in order to determine whether . . . [there is] discrimination, we would need to know what proportion of all capital crimes are committed by blacks." Some FBI reports suggest that about 57 percent of those arrested for deliberately killing

A condemned black man, noose around his neck, has only seconds before he dies on the gallows. Statistics show that members of minority races are executed in greater proportions than whites.

someone are black. This, Carrington concludes, may be one reason for the high proportion of blacks on death row.

Other researchers, however, suggest other reasons for the disproportionate numbers. Chief among them is the belief that blacks have historically received harsher sentences than whites for the same crimes. This is especially true, some say, in the case of the death penalty. Between 1930 and 1976, for example, a majority of rapes in the United States were committed by whites. Yet of the 455 people executed for rape during that period, 405 or about 90 percent were black. Rape is no longer punishable by death unless it occurs during a murder, so more recent statistics are unavailable. Nevertheless, of the more than 3,860 people executed for a range of crimes in the United States between 1930 and 1992, more than half were black.

Differing views

The race of the defendant has played a key role in sentencing decisions, many death penalty opponents state. The Massachusetts Labor Committee, an organization that published data and opinions about capital punishment in 1982, expressed this view:

> From the founding of this country until today, capital punishment has been an instrument of racism. Black people constitute about 12% of the population and 41% of the death row population. Study after study has substantiated the existence of racial discrimination and proven that race is, indeed, a key variable in sentencing.

This sort of evidence convinced the U.S. Supreme Court to state in 1972 that capital punishment was unconstitutional because it discriminated racially. In 1976, however, the Court ruled that the penalty could be used if a state passed and enforced laws against such discrimination. One former Supreme Court justice, Abe Fortas, felt that laws of this sort would be difficult or even impossible to enforce. Jurors, he suggested, could claim their decision for the death penalty was based on the evidence even if it was actually based on the defendant's race. Fortas later wrote, "All of the standards that can be devised to compel juries to impose the death penalty on capital offenders without exception or discrimination will be of no avail."

Another Supreme Court justice, Lewis F. Powell Jr., disagreed. In the 1980s, he stated that racial differences in the United States as a whole had decreased in the years following the adoption of civil rights legislation in the 1960s. Also, said Powell, while blacks and other minorities rarely sat on juries before the civil rights movement of

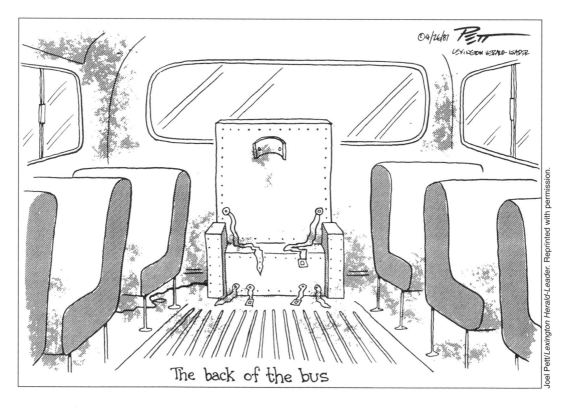

The back of the bus

the 1960s, they did so regularly by the 1980s. Because of these factors, he said:

> The possibility of racial bias in the trial and sentencing process has diminished in recent years. The segregation [separation of races] of our society in decades past, which contributed substantially to the severity of punishment for interracial crimes, is now no longer prevalent in this country. Likewise, the day is past when juries do not represent the minority group elements of the community.

The McCleskey case

Powell's opinions about discrimination in capital punishment proved to be controversial when the issue came before the Supreme Court again in 1987. The issue arose in the case of Warren McCleskey, a black Georgia inmate appealing his death sentence on grounds of race discrimination. The case is important because it clearly illustrates how difficult it is to prove that a person received the death penalty because of his or her race.

In 1978, McCleskey took part in the armed robbery of an Atlanta furniture store. While the robbery was taking place, a policeman arrived at the store. He was shot and killed by one of the robbers. Whether McCleskey fired the fatal shot was never proved, but under Georgia law he was still guilty of murder. He was convicted and sentenced to death. Out of seventeen people charged with killing a police officer in Fulton County, Georgia, between 1973 and 1980, McCleskey, a black man who had killed a white man, was the only one to be sentenced to death. This fact attracted the attention of the National Association for the Advancement of Colored People, which supported McCleskey's appeal that he had been sentenced to death because he was black. The case went all the way to the U.S Supreme Court.

McCleskey's lawyers presented a great deal of

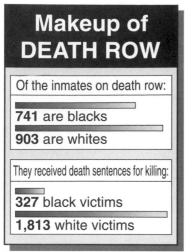

Makeup of DEATH ROW

Of the inmates on death row:

741 are blacks

903 are whites

They received death sentences for killing:

327 black victims

1,813 white victims

Source: NAACP Legal Defense and Educational Fund Inc.

statistical evidence to support their claims, including the most in-depth study ever done about the use of the death penalty in a state. Much of their evidence was based on studies done by Professor David Baldus of the University of Iowa in Iowa City. Baldus examined 2,484 cases of murder that occurred in Georgia between 1973 and 1979. He found that 22 percent of the blacks who killed whites were sentenced to death. Yet only 3 percent of the whites who killed blacks received the death penalty. Eleven convicted killers were actually executed, and nine of them were black. After much careful study, Baldus concluded that race was the primary factor influencing these death penalty sentences. The race of the defendant and the race of the victim both seemed to play a role in sentencing.

Citing Baldus's study, McCleskey's lawyers argued that a clear pattern of racial bias in death penalty sentences existed in Georgia. Until state authorities eliminated this problem, they said, it was unfair to impose the death penalty in Georgia.

Difficult proof

But the Supreme Court disagreed and upheld McCleskey's death sentence. The majority of justices said that McCleskey had provided insufficient evidence of any "intentional discrimination" against him. Basically, the Court's decision maintained that statistics—even if they showed a general pattern of discrimination—did not prove that McCleskey's sentence specifically resulted from discrimination. It was not enough, the justices said, for McCleskey to show that a pattern of discrimination existed. For McCleskey's sentence to be reversed, McCleskey would have to prove that he had actually been sentenced to die because of his race. This meant that he and others who felt their death sentences had been influenced by race would have to show that a specific prosecutor, sentencing judge, or jury was racially biased in calling for and imposing the death penalty.

This type of proof is difficult to obtain, much more difficult than showing a pattern of bias occurring over time. Nevertheless, this ruling set the standard for McCleskey and all appeals similar to his.

After the ruling the ACLU said:

> The difficult standard of proof required by the court virtually insures that most death sentences which result from *system-wide* discrimination will not be remedied. Only in the rare case when a defendant can prove what went on in the minds of a prosecutor, judge or jury member would a capital defendant be protected against race discrimination.

The worth of the victim

Opponents of the death penalty believe that judges and jurors may be influenced by the defendant's race. They may also be affected by the victim's race. In his studies of the death penalty in Georgia, Baldus discovered that the race of the crime victim had a great bearing on the severity of the defendant's sentence. According to Baldus and other researchers, some murder victims may be seen as better or more valuable than others. And the killers of those seen as more valuable frequently receive harsher sentences. In Georgia, Baldus found, many whites think of blacks as less valuable than whites. His study revealed that 87 percent of the death sentences imposed in Georgia were for cases involving a white victim. It was eleven times more likely, he found, for the death penalty to be imposed in white-victim cases than in black-victim cases.

Historically, similar patterns have occurred in other states. Between 1974 and 1977, 173 Ohio murder cases involved blacks killing whites.

Twenty-five percent of the defendants received the death penalty. In the same period, forty-seven cases involved whites murdering blacks. None of the whites were sentenced to die. In Florida, Texas, and Georgia, 842 black people were convicted of murdering whites between 1973 and 1977. Of these, 16 percent received the death penalty. In the same period, 294 whites were convicted of killing blacks, and only 1 percent of them received death sentences.

More recently, the U.S. General Accounting Office, or GAO, conducted a nationwide study of the death penalty in 1990. The study found similar patterns of discrimination in many states. Reported the GAO, "Those who murdered whites were found to be more likely to be sentenced to death than those who murdered blacks."

Misinterpretation of the law

Concern over discrimination against non-white defendants in death penalty cases was roused again in 1991. The object of this concern was a Supreme Court ruling that allows judges and juries to consider a victim's worth in deciding the sentence to be imposed on the person convicted of the crime. U.S. attorney general Dick Thornburgh represented the Bush administration's position that victim worth should be considered.

A victim's worth, said Thornburgh, might be based on such factors as his or her high standing in the community or the fact that he or she was the sole support of many children. The Bush administration did not intend for jurors to discriminate racially or otherwise when considering the worth of a victim. The idea was to make it tougher on murderers by raising their chances of getting the death penalty. This would be accomplished, officials said, by allowing judges and juries to know how the victim's death affected a family or even a community. Also, the administration hoped, if more murderers were executed, more people would be deterred from committing murder.

Death penalty opponents immediately expressed concern over the ruling. They fear that

In 1991, U.S. attorney general Dick Thornburgh argued that juries should consider the victim's worth when sentencing murderers. Thornburgh's intent was to deter would-be murderers by more frequently imposing the death penalty.

Three black death row inmates play cards through their cell bars in Florida State Prison. Death penalty opponents contend that the possibility of discrimination in sentencing murderers to death is enough reason to ban capital punishment.

some jurors who might not have discriminated before now may feel freer to do so. And because there is little or no way to prove discrimination, such cases will be hard to appeal. Those who express this concern believe that a better way exists to eliminate various kinds of discrimination in imposing capital punishments. That way is to outlaw the death penalty altogether.

To abolish or not to abolish?

Those against capital punishment say that any chance of discrimination is too much. They say that the only way the penalty could be administered fairly would be if all people were treated equally, both in society and under the law. According to this view, since such equality does not exist, the death penalty should be abolished. This was the argument used by the House Committee of the District of Columbia, a government group that studied the use of the death penalty in the 1970s. Reported the committee:

> As it is now applied, the death penalty is nothing but an arbitrary discrimination against an occasional victim. . . . Almost any criminal with influence or wealth can escape it, but the poor and friendless convict . . . [or the member of a racial minority] is the one singled out as a sacrifice to what is no more than tradition.

However, many death penalty advocates argue that the existence of discrimination is not reason enough to outlaw capital punishment. They point out that abolishing the death penalty will allow *all* who commit serious crimes to escape the punishment they deserve. Ernest van den Haag writes:

> If and when discrimination occurs it should be corrected. Not, however, by letting the guilty blacks escape the death penalty because guilty whites do, but by making sure that the guilty white offenders suffer it as the guilty blacks do. Discrimination must be abolished by abolishing discrimination—not by abolishing penalties. However, even if one assumes that this cannot be done, I do not see any good reason to let any guilty murderer escape his penalty. It does happen in the administration of criminal justice that one person gets away with murder and another is executed. Yet the fact that one gets away with it is no reason to let another one escape.

Thus, there is still much disagreement over the extent of discrimination in death penalty sentencing. All responsible members of the legal community agree that such bias, if and when it exists, is wrong. If the death penalty must be used, say both its advocates and opponents, it should be used fairly. But the two sides continue to disagree over whether it should be used at all.

5

Juveniles on Death Row

THE EXECUTION OF juveniles, or people younger than age eighteen, stirs people's emotions like few other topics. As New York City attorney Glenn M. Bieler comments:

> Juvenile capital punishment has become one of the major controversial issues to unfold in the last decade. This issue adds a new dimension to the emotional debates surrounding the death penalty.

Understanding the consequences

At the core of this controversy is the question of whether juveniles are capable of fully understanding the consequences of their actions. Many people feel they are not, and, therefore, should not face punishments as severe as those given to adults. "The notion that young people should not suffer the death penalty," states Amnesty International, "stems from the recognition that they are not fully mature—hence not fully responsible. . . ." Those who express this opinion also believe that juvenile offenders stand a good chance of turning their lives around. They are still in the formative stages, both mentally and emotionally. They may be rehabilitated, or taught constructive ways of living and behaving in society.

Other people reject these ideas. They say that,

(Opposite page) A young inmate on death row peers anxiously through the bars of his cell— perhaps the last home he will know. The debate over the death penalty heats up when juvenile killers are the subject.

61

despite their age and level of maturity, juveniles should be held as accountable as adults for the crimes they commit. Young people—like adults—are capable of committing horrible crimes. This is evident from their numbers on death row. In December 1991, for example, 36 of the nation's 2,547 death-row inmates had received death sentences for crimes they committed before the age of eighteen. Specific examples also show that young people are capable of horrible crimes. For instance, in December 1982, seventeen-year-old George Burns Jr., shot his father six times in the back of the head in the living

Many people believe that young people are not fully mature, and are therefore incapable of understanding the consequences of their actions.

room of their Jacksonville, Florida, home. In November 1981, Anthony Jacques Broussard, sixteen, strangled his fourteen-year-old girlfriend to death in Milpitas, California. His friends helped him hide her body, and no one told the authorities for two days.

Those who support the death penalty for juveniles say that in brutal cases like these, society should focus on the crime, and not the age of the offender. Wrote Rodger A. Maynes in the *Journal of Juvenile Law*, a publication of the University of La Verne College of Law, in La Verne, California:

> The acts of wanton killing and brutality committed by young people must be effectively combatted. There is an immediate, though certainly not ideal, solution to the problem. That solution consists of holding certain "hard-core" juvenile offenders to stand trial and be punished as adults. . . . When such a juvenile . . . stands trial as an adult, then society should be allowed to impose any appropriate sanction, including death.

An emotional issue

All through the 1970s and 1980s, legal and human rights groups urged the U.S. Supreme Court to ban juvenile executions. These groups argued that young people do not understand the consequences of their actions the same way adults do. Therefore, execution is too harsh a punishment for juveniles. Such executions, said Amnesty and the ACLU, violate the Eighth Amendment of the Constitution which bans "cruel and unusual" punishment.

This argument failed to convince the Supreme Court, however. In June 1989, the Court ruled that executing youths under the age of eighteen is neither cruel nor unusual. The ruling arose from two murder cases. One involved a seventeen-year-old youth who sexually assaulted and then shot in the head a female gas station attendant

during a 1981 robbery. The other involved a sixteen-year-old youth who repeatedly stabbed a woman convenience store owner in the neck and chest during a 1985 robbery.

The Court's majority opinion took the position that society sets a standard for what is considered cruel and unusual. State laws are one indication of that standard. At the time of the ruling, the justices said, the laws in states nationwide did not indicate that the public considered execution of juvenile offenders cruel or unusual.

Supreme Court justice Antonin Scalia emphasized this point in the Court's majority opinion. He calculated that only twelve of thirty-seven states that permitted capital punishment in 1989 actually prohibited a death sentence for offenders under eighteen. Three other states, he said, prohibited the death penalty for those under seventeen. "This does not establish the degree of national consensus this Court has previously thought sufficient to label a particular punishment cruel and unusual," Scalia concluded.

Troubled backgrounds

The Court's decision highlighted an important aspect of the debate over executing juveniles. This is the question of whether a young person's background should be taken into account in the decision to impose the death penalty. Many juveniles involved in violent crimes have troubled backgrounds. Often, they have suffered years of physical and emotional abuse. Because they are still young, they have not developed the maturity required to solve problems in a reasonable, peaceful manner. When upset or angry, they strike out at people and at society in general.

Social workers Elizabeth Lyttleton Sturz and Mary Taylor believe that such young criminals can still be saved. They write:

Justice Antonin Scalia of the U.S. Supreme Court wrote the 1989 majority opinion which held that executing juveniles was not considered by the American public to be cruel and unusual punishment.

> The problem is huge and complicated, of course. But our experience has shown that angry, alienated teenagers can be pulled in, can be brought to the point where they not only do not steal and assault but have something of value to give to society. The message to these teenagers has to be: You are valuable, society cares about you. You have the obligation and the resources to reach your potential.

Researchers have found that many violent offenders, but especially those who commit murder in their teens, have suffered physical and mental abuse from an early age. Studies such as the one conducted in the mid-1980s by psychiatrist Dorothy Lewis of the New York University School of Medicine prompt calls for mercy in the face of circumstances beyond a child's control.

Lewis and her colleagues interviewed fourteen young offenders on death row. All fourteen had been sentenced to death for a murder committed before reaching the age of eighteen. The survey participants included seven whites, six blacks, and one Latino.

The researchers hoped to learn what the link might be between the offenders' backgrounds and the crimes they had committed. What the researchers found was that all fourteen offenders had suffered serious head injuries as children. All but two had been severely beaten or physically abused. Five had been sexually abused by relatives. Nine of the fourteen showed serious brain abnormalities, including seizures and actual brain damage. Seven were psychotic, consistently unable to distinguish reality from fantasy. And four others had frequent and violent mood changes. The other three suffered from an intense fear that someone was going to attack or persecute them. Almost all came from families with histories of alcoholism, drug abuse, and psychiatric problems.

"Violence begets violence"

Summing up the study, Don Colburn of the *Washington Post* wrote, "All [of those studied] had serious psychiatric problems, and most had brain abnormalities, low IQs and poor mental test scores." The study concluded that juveniles who are sentenced to death in the United States usually have many emotional and psychological problems. One doctor involved in the study, Jonathan H. Pincus, remarked:

> The finding is . . . very much at odds with . . . [the traditional view] which is that criminals are criminals and there's nothing wrong with . . . [their brains or mental conditions].

If almost all of these young criminals are mentally impaired, it raises questions about whether they should receive the same punishments as

criminals who are not impaired. "The findings," says Colburn, "support the conclusion that violence begets violence—and abuse, abuse."

The Heath Wilkins case

Many who agree with the conclusion that violence begets violence cite as an example the case of Heath Wilkins. On July 27, 1985, sixteen-year-old Wilkins stabbed and killed Nancy Allen, a twenty-seven-year-old liquor store clerk, during a robbery attempt in Avondale, Missouri. In 1986, Wilkins was convicted and sentenced to die. The jury decided that Wilkins had committed an adult crime, so he should receive an adult punishment. Wilkins's lawyers argued that their client's abnormal, abusive background should be considered in sentencing. Because Wilkins himself was a victim to be pitied, they maintained, he should re-

Juveniles can commit brutal murders. Many people believe such acts should be punished with death regardless of who commits them.

Convicted of a violent murder committed when he was sixteen, Heath Wilkins is under a death sentence. His defenders argue that his crime was a result of childhood abuse and that he deserves a more merciful punishment.

ceive imprisonment rather than the death penalty.

An examination of Wilkins's background reveals that his troubles began when he was very young. According to Sean O'Brien, chief of the public defender's office in Kansas City, Missouri, Wilkins was an abused and self-destructive child. When Wilkins was three or four years old, a male babysitter sexually abused him. Later, he was repeatedly beaten by one of his mother's boyfriends. At age five, an adult relative fed him drugs. As such abuse continued, Wilkins started inhaling gasoline fumes because they caused hallucinations and, therefore, made him forget his troubles. High concentrations of these fumes cause brain damage. Wilkins claimed he did this at least five hundred times during his elementary school years. Eventually, he got in trouble with the law, his mother lost custody of him, and he began living on the streets.

Sean O'Brien, who represented Wilkins in his sentencing appeals, claimed his client was in a psychotic state, meaning he was unable to sense reality, when he committed the crime. Therefore, Wilkins should have been given a chance for rehabilitation rather than death by execution. Larry Harman, who prosecuted Wilkins, disagreed, saying that Wilkins should be executed for his crime. Harman believes that, regardless of his serious childhood problems, Wilkins knew what he was doing when he stabbed Nancy Allen. According to the letter of the law, Harman believes, as long as a murderer is aware of committing the act, he or she can and should be convicted and punished for the crime. And if the law sets the punishment as death, then the murderer should die, even if he or she is a juvenile.

Protecting minors

The abusive background of offenders is just one aspect of the debate about juveniles on death row. There is also the issue of what legal authorities call *parens patria*. This is the long-recognized principle that society should afford special protection to minors. It was summed up by the Supreme Court in a 1979 decision. That decision said that

> . . . [states] may limit the freedom of children to choose for themselves in the making of important, affirmative choices with potentially serious consequences. . . . During the formative years of childhood and adolescence, minors often lack the experience, perspective, and judgment to recognize and avoid choices that could be detrimental [harmful] to them.

This difficulty in making decisions, says death penalty opponent Glenn Bieler, is the reason society does not allow people under eighteen to

Society considers juveniles too immature to vote, buy liquor, serve on juries, or join the armed forces. When it comes to murder, however, many people believe juveniles should be punished as adults—even if that means death.

vote. They are also considered too young to serve as jurors, join the armed forces, or buy liquor. Bieler contends:

> The premise behind such deprivations [restrictions] is that minors are not possessed with the full capacity to make individual choices. Therefore, it is difficult to understand how states can execute minors. Can a state at one moment say that minors are incapable of making adult decisions, then at the next moment say that minors should be held as responsible as adults for their acts?

Judge the individual

Ernest van den Haag's answer to this question is yes, at least sometimes. Van den Haag believes that each case should be examined separately. Some people are educated and mature enough to vote at age thirteen, while others at age twenty-

Chuck Asay, by permission of the *Colorado Springs Gazette Telegraph.*

one are not. The same thing is true, he says, in criminal cases.

> Each case is different. While some juvenile murderers are quite immature, others are quite mature. Our criminal justice system accommodates those differences. In capital trials . . . the jury weighs the . . . [various] factors. . . . Surely, if the jury feels that the juvenile murderer did not understand the meaning of the act, the jury will not impose the death penalty. But it is simply unrealistic and silly to insist that no one under eighteen can be held fully accountable.

The debate about executing juveniles goes on. The arguments are often emotional, perhaps because most people are sensitive to topics relating to young people. Young people, after all, represent society's future. Traditionally, childhood and adolescence are seen as periods when young people make mistakes, then correct them in preparation for adulthood. The question remains, should juveniles suffer the ultimate penalty for the worst of those mistakes?

Is the Death Penalty Morally Right?

AMONG ALL THE issues surrounding the death penalty, the question of whether it is moral is perhaps the most basic. The issues of deterrence, executing innocents, discrimination in sentencing, and executing juveniles revolve around the effectiveness, fairness, and legality of the death penalty. The morality issue involves one overriding and rather simple question: Is capital punishment right or wrong? People are sharply divided on this question.

Heartfelt expressions

Many people have strong feelings about the morality of capital punishment. One such person was Andrei Sakharov, a Russian scholar and winner of the Nobel Peace prize. Sakharov often spoke out against the use of capital punishment by his own or any other country. Said Sakharov:

> I regard the death penalty as a savage and immoral institution which undermines the moral and legal foundation of society. A state . . . takes upon itself the right to the most terrible and irreversible act— the deprivation of life. Such a state cannot expect an improvement of the moral atmosphere in its

(Opposite page) A sign carried by a child in a demonstration against the death penalty points out the finality of capital punishment. Many people question whether executions by the state are any less immoral than murder.

Eminent Russian scholar Andrei Sakharov believed that the death penalty is immoral and only begets violence in society.

country. I reject the notion that the death penalty has any essential deterrent effect on potential offenders. I am convinced that the contrary is true—that savagery begets only savagery.

Those who see the death penalty as moral are just as passionate in expressing their beliefs. Award-winning Chicago journalist Mike Royko strongly defends the death penalty. As he puts it:

> When I think of the thousands of inhabitants of Death Rows in the hundreds of prisons in this country . . . My reaction is: What's taking us so long? Let's get that electrical current flowing. Drop those pellets [of poison gas] now! Whenever I argue this with friends who have opposite views, they say that I don't have enough regard for that most marvelous of miracles—human life. Just the opposite: It's because I have so much regard for human life that I favor capital punishment. Murder is the most terrible crime there is. Anything less than the death penalty is an insult to the victim and society. It says, in effect, that we don't value the victim's life enough to punish the killer fully.

Strong opinions like those of Sakharov and Royko are the fuel for continuous debates, both public and private, about the morality of the death penalty. These debates most often divide into four basic areas: human rights, the right of the state to kill, revenge, and excessive cruelty.

Human rights

Most people agree that a human life is special and that a human being has certain basic rights. Perhaps the most important of these rights is the right to live out one's life. But there is considerable disagreement about whether a murderer deserves to keep this right.

In a free society, most people understand that those who commit crimes may be deprived of certain rights or freedoms. A person who robs a bank, for example, may be sent to prison, thus losing the right to live freely. When a person kills another, that person may also lose certain rights and freedoms. Among those lost rights, some people believe, should be the right to continue living.

By taking a life, the murderer forfeits the right to his or her own life, Ernest van den Haag says. He adds:

> To insist that the murderer has the same right to live as his victim pushes . . . [the idea of equal inborn rights] too far. . . . His crime morally sets the murderer apart from his victim. The victim did, and therefore the murderer does not, deserve to live. His life cannot be sacred if that of his victim was.

In van den Haag's view, society has the responsibility of protecting the sacredness of life by punishing those who willfully destroy it:

> One may well argue that human life is cheapened when murderers, instead of being executed, are imprisoned as pickpockets are. It is not enough to proclaim human life . . . [sacred]. Innocent life is best secured by telling those who would take it that they will forfeit their own life.

Not everyone agrees with this point of view, however. Some people believe that no crime, no matter how brutal, cancels a person's right to con-

Chuck Asay, by permission of the *Colorado Springs Gazette Telegraph.*

Demonstrators staged a candlelight vigil in Columbia, South Carolina, in 1986 to protest a scheduled execution.

tinue living. Even those who commit murder and other serious crimes retain this basic right. To deny this, Amnesty International says, is to deny the very idea that a human being has certain basic rights. "The idea that a government can justify a punishment as cruel as death conflicts with the very concept of human rights," Amnesty says. "The significance of human rights is precisely that some means may never be used to protect society because their use violates the very values which make society worth protecting."

In other words, society cannot say it upholds human rights while it denies some people the most basic of those rights. Amnesty continues:

> Central to fundamental human rights, is that they are inalienable. They may not be taken away even if a person has committed the most atrocious of crimes. Human rights apply to the worst of us as well as to the best of us, which is why they protect all of us.

Former Supreme Court justice William Brennan agrees. He sees each individual as possessing a basic worth, a value he calls simple human dignity. This value, Brennan says, is innate, or inborn, and cannot be given or taken away by the state or anyone else. In Brennan's view, a person who commits a terrible crime does so for various reasons that society may or may not excuse. But these reasons are influenced by social and environmental factors and have nothing to do with the person's basic worth. Brennan says:

> The calculated killing of a human by the state involves, by its very nature, an absolute denial of the executed person's humanity. The most vile murder does not, in my view, release the state from constitutional restraints on the destruction of human dignity.

Murder by the state

Capital punishment has, in fact, been characterized by many people as state-sanctioned murder. If killing is wrong, these people argue, then killing by the state is also wrong. "An execution cannot be used to condemn killing; it *is* killing," Amnesty International says. "Such an act by the state is the mirror image of the criminal's willingness to use physical violence against a victim."

Equally disturbing to many death penalty opponents is the government's role as executioner. Many question whether a government should engage in the act of killing, especially for reasons other than war. Says John Gabriel Healey, executive director of Amnesty International U.S.A.:

> The basic obligation of governments is to protect people, not to destroy them. Governments whose business is to kill are violating the basic reasons of why they are there. If a state can kill its citizens, it can do anything else to its citizens. . . . So what you must do to protect the fabric of society is keep governments out of the business of killing their citizens.

Yet governments frequently must use many different tools to protect their citizens. Strict laws

Death penalty supporters make their feelings known on the subject of Robert Alton Harris's execution at California's San Quentin prison.

regarding life and death are but one of these tools. Through laws, a government and its citizens create a contract which they hope will work for the good of everyone. That contract contains certain penalties that will be imposed if the contract is broken. When an individual breaks the law, he or she violates the contract and must submit to those penalties. Writer Walter Burns believes capital punishment is an effective tool for enforcing moral order. "Capital punishment," he writes, "serves to remind us of the majesty of the moral order that is embodied in our law, and of the terrible consequences of its breach."

An expression of moral outrage

Capital punishment is also described by some as a natural expression of moral social anger at a horrible act. In his book *Due Process of Law*, Joel M. Gora states:

Capital punishment is an expression of society's moral outrage at particularly offensive conduct. The [execution] may be unappealing to many, but it is essential in an ordered society. . . . Indeed, the decision that capital punishment may be the appropriate sanction [penalty] in extreme cases is an expression of the community's belief that certain crimes are themselves so . . . [terrible] that the only adequate response may be the penalty of death.

The strongest expressions of emotion usually come, not surprisingly, from family and friends of murder victims. Often they have little patience for philosophical debates over a state's responsibility to its citizens or a killer's human rights. They know only that a cherished family member or friend died at the brutal hand of another. In 1992, a Milwaukee, Wisconsin, court convicted mass murderer Jeffrey Dahmer of killing fifteen people. Wisconsin has no death penalty, and Dahmer received a life sentence for his horrible crimes. At the end of the trial, family members of Dahmer's victims rose one by one to speak to him. Many

Jeffrey Dahmer commited some of the most gruesome murders in U.S. history. He was sentenced to life imprisonment because Wisconsin, the site of his crimes, has no death penalty. Some death penalty advocates claim the families of Dahmer's victims were cheated because Dahmer's life was not taken in return.

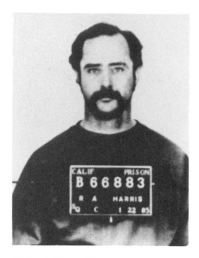

Robert Alton Harris was executed in April 1992, fourteen years after he murdered two young men in California. The relatives of the victims feel that justice has finally been done.

said that they wished he could be executed, their voices quavering with anger and anguish.

Strong emotions were also expressed by family members of two young men murdered in California in 1978 by Robert Alton Harris. Harris's appeals process lasted fourteen years before the state finally executed him in April 1992. Marilyn Clark, the sister of John Mayeski, one of Robert Alton Harris's victims, continues to visit her brother's grave twice a week after thirteen years. She says:

> It's a constant upbringing of memories, of feelings of loss, of what we could have had. John could have had a family. His children could have been playing with mine right now. The things we've lost over the years, that's what hurts. It's a constant reminder.

Outrage and feelings of revenge by the family and friends of a murder victim are understandable. But should these feelings, motivated by extreme grief and anger, guide society's response to murder? Former U.S. attorney general Ramsey Clark feels they should not. "Our emotions may cry out for vengeance in the wake of a horrible

In April 1992, as time grows short for condemned murderer Robert Alton Harris, emotions rise as demonstrators on opposite sides of the issue clash.

"MAYBE THIS WILL TEACH YOU THAT IT'S MORALLY WRONG TO KILL PEOPLE!"

crime," he says, "but we know that killing the criminal cannot undo the crime." Adds Clark, execution "will not prevent similar crimes by others, does not benefit the victim, destroys human life and brutalizes society."

According to this view, capital punishment is the enactment of an "eye for an eye" philosophy, one that demands the taking of one life to make up for the taking of another. In other words, society demands retribution, or payment of some kind, from those who commit murder. "What the argument for retribution boils down to is often no more than a desire for vengeance masked as a principle of justice," says Amnesty International. From this viewpoint, the death penalty as an act of vengeance is wrong also because it sets a poor example for selecting punishment. If taking one life to avenge another is just, then society should repay each crime with a like punishment. Most legal systems today reject such an approach to punishment. As Amnesty puts it:

> If today's penal systems do not sanction the burning of an arsonist's home, the rape of a rapist or the torture of a torturer, it is not because they tolerate the crimes. Instead, it is because societies understand that they must be built on a different set of values from those they condemn.

However, some people do not accept the idea that the death penalty is a form of vengeance. Said Robert E. Crowe, former state attorney for Cook County, Illinois:

> Instead, capital punishment is a form of protection for society by permanently removing a killer from that society. Murderers are not punished for revenge. The man with the life blood of another upon his hands is a menace to the life of every citizen. He should be removed from society for the sake of society. In his removal, society is sufficiently protected, but only provided it is a permanent removal.

This permanent removal is, of course, the execution of the criminal. To some people, executions are not only permanent, but also excessively brutal. They believe that capital punishment, despite the U.S. Supreme Court's view, does constitute "cruel and unusual punishment." Execution, they say, is a form of cruelty second to none and is, therefore, immoral.

A continuing debate

Most citizens have never witnessed an execution. If they had, Amnesty International's John Healey says, they would probably agree that executions are barbaric. "In each case a government has decided that it has the right to remove a selected individual not merely from society but from life itself. In each case, the method is cruel, inhuman and degrading," Healey says.

By contrast, there are those who feel that the horrifying aspects of executions are part of what make the death penalty a deterrent against murder. They say that fear of such horrors makes people think twice about killing someone and, therefore, executions are moral. Walter Berns says:

> The criminal law [and its penalties] must be made awful, by which I mean inspiring, or commanding 'profound respect or . . . fear.' It must remind us of the moral order by which alone we can live as *human* beings . . .

Such forceful and emotional opinions on the morality of state executions illustrate the continuing heated debate about capital punishment. These opinions are largely expressions of feelings that come from the heart and are, therefore, very strong. That is one important reason that society remains so divided about capital punishment.

Yet interestingly, many people are not so solidly for or against the various issues surrounding the death penalty. They often empathize with positions on both sides. In fact, public surveys indicate that a majority of people in the United States see merit on both sides of many death penalty issues. Thus, general agreement about the use of the death penalty is not likely to come for a very long time, if ever. For the present, every citizen has a duty to be as informed as possible about the subject of capital punishment. Whether effective or ineffective, moral or immoral, the death penalty is enacted in the name of every citizen. It is, therefore, everyone's responsibility.

Glossary

acquittal: In a trial, finding that the accused person is not guilty of the charges.

capital offense: A crime punishable by death.

circumstantial evidence: Indirect evidence of a fact at issue, based on related events or circumstances.

commutation: In sentencing, the reduction of a sentence to a less severe punishment.

constitutionality: Being in accordance with the rules and principles set out by the U.S. Constitution or an individual state constitution.

crime of passion: A crime committed by a person who is emotionally upset, enraged, or temporarily out of control.

defendant: The person in a trial who has been accused of committing a crime.

deterrence: The prevention of an act because of fear.

forgery: Making false documents.

homicide: Murder.

juvenile: A person under the age of eighteen.

moratorium: A temporary suspension of specifically designated activities.

ordinary crimes: Usually defined as nonmilitary or nonwartime offenses.

***parens patria*:** The principle that society should afford special protection to minors.

prosecutor: The lawyer who argues the case for the state against a criminal.

rehabilitation: The process of training someone to think and act more constructively.

retribution: Payment made to a victim or society for the commission of a crime.

treason: Betraying one's country.

Organizations
to Contact

American Bar Association (ABA)
750 N. Lake Shore Dr.
Chicago, IL 60611
(312) 988-5000

The ABA, the foremost legal organization in the United States, works to improve the civil and criminal justice systems. The organization opposes the death penalty for mentally retarded murderers and those under eighteen. The ABA conducts research and educational programs and publishes the *ABA Newsletter* and the monthly *ABA Journal*.

American Civil Liberties Union (ACLU) Capital Punishment Project
122 Maryland Ave. NE
Washington, DC 20002
(202) 234-4890

Founded in 1920, the ACLU champions the rights set forth in the Declaration of Independence and the Constitution. The union is one of America's oldest civil liberties organizations. Staunch opponents of the death penalty, members of the union defend death row inmates and attempt to postpone executions. The ACLU publishes the quarterly newspaper *Civil Liberties* and various pamphlets, books, and position papers.

American Correctional Associations (ACA)
8025 Laurel Lakes Ct.
Laurel, MD 20707
(301) 206-5100

The ACA is an organization of corrections professionals, including prison wardens and parole officers. It works to improve prison and correctional standards by providing information on the practical aspects of criminal justice, including the effectiveness of punishments such as the death penalty. The association publishes books and the monthly periodical *Corrections Today.*

Americans for Effective Law Enforcement (AELE)
5519 N. Cumberland Ave. #1008
Chicago, IL 60656-1471
(312) 763-2800

AELE attempts to help prosecutors, police, and the courts promote fairer, more effective administration of criminal law and equal justice, including unbiased sentences for all criminals. Some of the organization's many monthly publications include *Jail and Prisoner Law Bulletin* and *Security Legal Update.*

Amnesty International U.S.A.
322 Eighth Ave.
New York, NY 10001
(212) 807-8400

Amnesty International is an international human rights organization that opposes the death penalty. Among Amnesty's many publications on the death penalty are the pamphlet *The Death Penalty: Cruel and Unusual Punishment* and the book *A Punishment In Search of a Crime.* The organization also publishes the bimonthly newsletter *Amnesty Action.*

The Heritage Foundation
214 Massachusetts Ave. NE
Washington, DC 20002
(202) 546-4400

The foundation is a public policy research institute that supports the death penalty to reduce and deter crime. Heritage Foundation publications include the pamphlet *A Note on the Sentencing of Criminals*, the quarterly journal *Policy Review*, and the periodic *Backgrounder* and *Heritage Lectures.*

The Lincoln Institute for Research and Education
1001 Connecticut Ave. NW, Suite 1135
Washington, DC 20036
(202) 223-5112

The Lincoln Institute studies public policy issues affecting black Americans. The institute, which supports the death penalty, sponsors conferences and publishes the *Lincoln Review*, a monthly journal of political and social opinion.

NAACP Legal Defense and Educational Fund
99 Hudson St., Suite 1600
New York, NY 10013
(212) 219-1900

The NAACP Legal Defense and Educational Fund is the legal branch of the National Association for the Advancement of Colored People. The fund opposes the death penalty and works to end discrimination in the criminal justice system. In addition to compiling statistics on the death penalty, the fund publishes legal materials, brochures, reports, and the quarterly *Equal Justice*.

National Center for Juvenile Justice
701 Forbes Ave.
Pittsburgh, PA 15219
(412) 227-6950

The National Center for Juvenile Justice compiles statistics on juvenile crime and punishment. The center does not take a stance on the death penalty for juveniles, but it provides information on the issue. It maintains research files and a library of one thousand volumes on juvenile justice and operates a resource center. In addition to monographs, reports, and studies, the center publishes the annuals *Today's Delinquent* and *Juvenile Court Statistics*.

National Coalition to Abolish the Death Penalty
1325 G St. NW, Lower Level B
Washington, DC 20005
(202) 347-2411

The National Coalition to Abolish the Death Penalty is a collection of more than 115 groups working together to stop executions in the United States. The organization compiles statistics on the death penalty. To further its goal, the coalition publishes *Legislative Action to Abolish the Death Penalty*, information packets, pamphlets, and research materials.

The Sentencing Project
918 F St. NW, Suite 501
Washington, DC 20005
(202) 628-0871

The Sentencing Project supports establishing and improving punishment alternatives to imprisonment and the death penalty. To promote its belief in alternative sentencing, the project sponsors seminars and speakers and publishes the annual *National Directory of Felony Sentencing Services*.

U.S. Department of Justice
Constitution Ave. and Tenth St.
Washington, DC 20530
(202) 514-2000

The Department of Justice compiles statistics on crime and the criminal justice system. Write for information and a list of publications.

Victims of Crime and Leniency (VOCAL)
PO Box 1283
114 N. Hull St.
Montgomery, AL 36103
(205) 262-7197

VOCAL, an organization of victims of crime, seeks to ensure that victims' rights are recognized and protected. It supports the death penalty and measures to reduce crime and increase punishment for criminals. VOCAL publications include the quarterly *VOCAL Voice* and a newsletter.

Washington Legal Foundation
1705 N St. NW
Washington, DC 20036
(202) 857-0240

The foundation is a legal research organization that represents crime victims seeking restitution. It supports the death penalty as a just punishment for murder. The foundation publishes the monograph *Capital Punishment* as well as the weekly *Legal Backgrounders* and the monthly *WLF Working Papers Studies*.

Suggestions for Further Reading

Hugo Adam Bedau, ed., *The Death Penalty in America*. New York: Oxford University Press, 1982.

Edmund G. ("Pat") Brown, with Dick Adler, *Public Justice and Private Mercy: A Governor's Education on Death Row*. London: Weidenfield and Nicholson, 1988.

Shirley Dicks, *Death Row: Interviews with Inmates, Their Families, and Opponents of Capital Punishment*. Jefferson, NC: McFarland & Co., 1990.

Thomas Draper, ed., *Capital Punishment*. New York: H. H. Wilson Company, 1985.

Michael E. Endres, *The Morality of Capital Punishment: Equal Justice Under the Law*. Mystic, CT: Twenty-third Publications, 1985.

Robert Johnson, *Condemned to Die: Life Under Sentence of Death*. New York: Elsevier North Holland, Inc., 1981.

Victor Streib, *Death Penalty for Juveniles*. Bloomington: Indiana University Press, 1987.

Carol Wekesser, ed., *The Death Penalty: Opposing Viewpoints*. San Diego: Greenhaven Press, 1991.

Works Consulted

Amnesty International, *When the State Kills . . . The Death Penalty: A Human Rights Issue*. New York: Amnesty International, U.S.A., 1989.

Kurt Anderson, "A 'More Palatable' Way of Killing," *Time*, December 20, 1982.

Kurt Anderson, "An Eye for an Eye," *Time*, January 24, 1983.

Hugo Adam Bedau, *The Case Against the Death Penalty*. New York: American Civil Liberties Union, 1984.

Eugene B. Block, *When Men Play God: The Fallacy of Capital Punishment*. San Francisco: Cragmont Publications, 1983.

Don Colburn, "Should We Execute Juvenile Killers?" *The Washington Post National Weekly Edition*, August 8-14, 1988.

Ian Gray and Maria Stanley, for Amnesty International, U.S.A., *A Punishment in Search of a Crime: Americans Speak Out Against the Death Penalty*. New York: Avon Books, 1989.

Elinor Lander Horwitz, *Capital Punishment, U.S.A.* Philadelphia: J. B. Lippincott Co., 1973.

David Margolick, "In the Land of the Death Penalty, Charges of Racism," *The New York Times,* July 10, 1991.

Louis P. Masur, *Rites of Execution: Capital Punishment and the Transformation of American Culture*. New York: Oxford University Press, 1989.

Gary E. McCuen and R.A. Baumgart, eds., *Reviving the Death Penalty*. Hudson, WI: Gem Publications, 1985.

David G. Savage, "Executing Young Killers Is Upheld," *The New York Times*, June 27, 1989.

Ernest van den Haag and John P. Conrad, *The Death Penalty: A Debate*. New York: Plenum Press, 1983.

D. B. Walker, "The Death Penalty: Legal Cruelty?" *USA Today*, November 1983.

William Wilbanks, *The Myth of a Racist Criminal Justice System*. Monterey, CA: Brooks/Cole Publishing, 1987.

Index

Alaska, abolition of death penalty, 19
Allen, Nancy, 67, 69
American Civil Liberties Union (ACLU), 45, 55, 63
American Revolution, 7
Amnesty International, 21, 41
  execution of juveniles and, 61, 63
  immorality of death penalties and, 76, 77, 81, 82

Babylonia, ancient, 11
Baldus, David, 54, 55
Beccaria, Cesare, 26
Berns, Walter, 83
Bible, 7, 11
Bieler, Glenn M., 61, 69-70
Bishop, Arthur Gary, 28
blacks
  murder arrests, 50-51
  on death row, 47, 49
  racial discrimination in sentencing, 51, 52-57, 59
  slaves, execution of, 12
Blackstone, William, 39, 40
Block, Eugene B., 35
Bonnet, Stede, 13
Brennan, William J., Jr., 76-77
Broussard, Anthony Jacques, 63
Burns, George, Jr., 62-63
Burns, Walter, 78
Bush, George, 16

Camus, Albert, 23
Canada, abolition of death penalty, 31-32
capital punishment, *see* death penalty
Carrington, Frank, 50-51

China, death penalty in, 20-21
civil rights movement, 52-53
Clark, Marilyn, 80
Clark, Ramsey, 80-81
Colburn, Don, 66-67
Conrad, John P., 30-31, 32
crime
  capital offenses, 11, 12-13
  federal law, 15-16
  international laws, 19-21
  political crimes, 20-21
  state laws, 16, 18
causes of
  crimes of passion, 32-33
  gang activity, 26, 31
  gun control and, 26, 27, 32
  poverty, 31, 48-49
death penalty and
  as retribution for, 18, 80-82
  brutalizing effect of, 35-37
  effectiveness as deterrence
    belief in, 16, 25, 74
    evidence against, 31-32, 33, 35
    evidence for, 27-29, 34
    execution moratorium and, 26-27, 30
    impossibility of, 22, 26, 73-74
    social and economic variables, 29-31
  juvenile offenses, 61-62, 63, 65, 66
public fears of, 16
punishment for
  "cruel and unusual" punishments, 63, 64-65, 82
  discrimination in, 11-12, 50-51, 55, 59
  human rights deprivation, 74-76, 77

proportionality in, 7, 81-82
victims of, 55, 57
wrongful convictions, 17-18, 39-41
Crowe, Robert E., 82
crucifixion, 13
cyanide gas, 14-15

Dahmer, Jeffrey, 79-80
Darwick, Norman, 25
death penalty
  abolition of
    international, 21-22, 23, 31-32
    state, 18-19
  as cause of murder, 36-37
  as murder, 8, 77
  as punishment
    appeals process, 17
    in ancient societies, 11-12, 13-14
    proportionality to crime, 7, 81-82
  brutalizing effect of, 35-36
  capital offenses, 11, 12-13
    federal law, 15-16
    international laws, 19-21
    state laws, 16, 18
  discrimination in application of, 11-12
    as reason for abolition, 57-59
    poverty and, 47-49
    race of defendants and, 47, 49-52, 53-55
    race of victims and, 53, 54, 55-57
    Supreme Court and, 47, 51-53, 54-55, 57
  effectiveness as deterrent, 37
    belief in, 16, 25, 57, 82-83
    evidence against, 31-33, 35
    evidence for, 27-29, 34
    impossibility of, 22, 26, 73-74
    measurement of, 26-27, 29-31, 34
  executions
    constitutional moratorium on, 26-27, 30, 51
    methods of, 13-15

number of, 18
of innocent person, 41
of juveniles, 61-62, 63, 67-68, 71
  as "cruel and unusual" punishment, 63, 64-65
morality of
  as moral anger, 78-80
  as morally wrong, 8-9, 22-23, 73-74, 82
  as respect for human life, 18, 74
  as retribution, 80-82
  deprivation of human rights, 74-77
  rights of governments and, 77-78
public opinion and, 16, 83
wrongful conviction and, 17-18, 42-44
  as necessary risk, 40-41, 44-45
  as unacceptable risk, 39, 45
  legal safeguards against, 39-41
death row
  juveniles on, 62
  minorities on, 47, 49, 51
  number of inmates, 17
Douglas, William O., 47
drawing and quartering, 14

electric chair, 14-15, 25
Endres, Michael, 47

Federal Bureau of Investigation (FBI), 50-51
firing squads, 15
Florida, death penalty in, 56
Fortas, Abe, 52
France
  abolition of death penalty, 23
  death penalty in, 14

gang violence, 26, 30, 31
Georgia, death penalty in, 53, 54, 55, 56
Gilmore, Gary, 28, 37
Gora, Joel M., 78-79
governments, right to kill, 77-78
Gray, Henry Judd, 8

Great Britain
  death penalty in, 12-13, 34, 35
  Parliament, 25
guillotine, 14
gun control, 26, 27, 32

Hammurabi (king of Babylonia),
  11, 12
handguns, 26
hanging, 15
Harman, Larry, 69
Harris, Robert Alton, 36, 78, 80
Healey, John Gabriel, 77, 82
Hebrews, ancient, 11
Horwitz, Elinor, 35
human rights, 74-77, 79
Hus, John, 12

India, ancient, 12
Iowa, abolition of death penalty,
  19
Iraq, death penalty in, 20-21

Japan, death penalty in, 21
Jordan, death penalty in, 20
juries, 52-53, 57-58
juveniles, 61-71

Kenya, death penalty in, 20
Kuwait, death penalty in, 21

Latinos, 47, 49
lawyers, 39-40, 48
Lee, Robert W., 28-29, 31
lethal injection, 15
Lewis, Dorothy, 65-66
life imprisonment, 8, 18
Lincoln, Abraham, 15
Los Angeles Police Department,
  34

McCleskey, Warren, 53-55
Massachusetts, abolition of death
  penalty, 19
Massachusetts Labor Committee,
  51
Mayeski, John, 80
Maynes, Rodger A., 63

Middle Ages, 14
Mill, John Stuart, 18, 40-41
minorities, 49
murder
  as capital offense, 12
    federal law, 15-16
    state laws, 16, 18, 64-65
  causes of, 26, 30-31, 32-33
    death penalty as, 36-37
    poverty as, 48-49
    race in, 50-51
  deterrence of
    effectiveness of death penalty
      belief in, 18, 25, 57, 82-83
      evidence against, 26, 29-30,
        31-33, 35
      evidence for, 27-29
    execution as, 8, 77
  juvenile offenders, 63-64, 65, 69,
    71
  punishment for
    as retribution, 79-82
    deprivation of right to live, 74-
      75, 76, 77
    proportionality in, 7, 82
    racial discrimination in, 54, 55-
      57
  U.S. rates of, 27
  victims of, 55, 57, 79, 80
  wrongful conviction for, 40-41

National Association for the
  Advancement of Colored People
  (NAACP), 53
New York (state), abolition of
  death penalty, 19, 20
New York Daily News, 8
Norway, abolition of death
  penalty, 23

O'Brien, Sean, 68, 69
Ohio, death penalty in, 55-56
Owens, Aaron, 41

parens patria, 69
Persia, ancient, 12
pickpocketing, 20, 34, 35
Pincus, Jonathan H., 66

Poland, death penalty in, 21
political crimes, 20-21
poverty, 31, 47, 48
Powell, Lewis F., Jr., 52-53

race riots, 31
racial discrimination, 51, 53-55, 57-59
rape, 16, 20, 51
religion, 12
Rhode Island, abolition of death penalty, 19
Richardson, James, 39, 42-44, 45
robbery, 20
Roberts, Dennis J., 19
Romania, death penalty in, 21
Rome, ancient, 13
Royko, Mike, 74

Sakharov, Andrei, 73-74
Scalia, Antonin, 64-65
Selby, Pierre Dale, 28
Siam, ancient, 13-14
slaves, execution of, 12
Snyder, Ruth Brown, 8
Sparta, death penalty in, 12
Spence, Karl, 27-28, 31
states
  death penalty laws, 15, 16-18
    abolition of, 18-19
    applied to juveniles, 64-65, 69-70
    effects on murder rates, 37
    moratorium on execution, 26-27
    racial discrimination in, 51-52
Steffen, Lloyd, 44
Sturz, Elizabeth Lyttleton, 65
suicide, 36
Switzerland, abolition of death penalty, 32

Taylor, Mary, 65
Texas, death penalty in, 56
Thornburgh, Dick, 57
Thurmond, Strom, 44-45
treason, 15, 19-20

United States, 18, 83

blacks executed in, 12, 49, 51
Congress, 16
  Senate, 44, 45
Constitution, Eighth Amendment, 63
death penalty and crime rates, 26-27
death row inmates, 49
execution methods, 14-15
federal death penalty, 7, 15-16, 19
General Accounting Office (GAO), 57
justice system, 39, 41-42
juveniles sentenced to death in, 66
murders in, 32
Supreme Court
  death penalties and, 82
    execution moratorium, 26-27, 47, 51
    juvenile executions, 63-65, 69
    racial discrimination in, 51-52, 53, 54-55, 57
Utah, death penalty in, 28-29, 30, 31

van den Haag, Ernest, 48-49, 59, 70-71, 75
Vietnam War, 31

West, Louis, 36
West Virginia, abolition of death penalty, 19
Wilkins, Heath, 67-69
Wisconsin, abolition of death penalty, 19, 79

Zehr, Howard, 26, 32-33, 35-36

About the Author

Don Nardo is an actor, film director, and composer as well as an award-winning writer. As an actor, he has appeared in more than fifty stage productions. He has also worked before or behind the camera in twenty films. Several of his musical compositions, including a young person's version of *The War of the Worlds* and the oratorio *Richard III*, have been played by regional orchestras. Mr. Nardo's writing credits include short stories, articles, and more than thirty-five books, including *Lasers; Voodoo; Anxiety and Phobias; The Irish Potato Famine; Exercise; Gravity; The Mexican-American War; Charles Darwin;* and *H.G. Wells*. Among his other writings are an episode of ABC's "Spenser: For Hire" and numerous screenplays. Mr. Nardo lives with his wife, Christine, on Cape Cod, Massachusetts.

Picture Credits